CEC SPECIAL EDUCATION ADVOCACY HANDBOOK

Developed by Jaclyn A. Bootel

The Department of Public Policy
Published by The Council for Exceptional Children

> *Note:* The references to either a male or female in this Handbook
> are meant to include both sexes.

Library of Congress Catalog Card Number: 94-73958

ISBN 0-86586-259-1

Copyright 1995 by The Council for Exceptional Children, 1920
Association Drive, Reston, Virginia 22091-1589.
(703) 620-3660
(703) 620-4334 (FAX)

Stock No. R5087 CEC Member Price $12.00; Regular Price $17.00

Printed in the United States of America
10 9 8 7 6 5 4 3 2 1

Contents

Foreword

The Council for Exceptional Children (CEC), as the largest professional organization representing those individuals dedicated to improving the educational outcomes for children and youth with disabilities and those who are gifted, is pleased to offer this first edition of the *CEC Special Education Advocacy Handbook,* which is going to be part of a complete training package developed to provide grassroots advocacy information directly to our CEC members.

According to the CEC Strategic Plan, "public policies at all levels of government are the underlying framework in serving individuals with exceptionalities and continually renewing our profession." CEC has a proud history as a force in the federal arena. We must strengthen this area and empower our members to be a force for meeting the policy challenges in the communities in which they live and work.

One of the main goals of the Strategic Plan is to "empower CEC members in all aspects of governmental/public policy through information, training and coordination of common agendas." This will be accomplished by the development and implementation of public policy training, including such resources as this *Handbook*.

As a special education professional, you already use elements of professional lobbying in your every day life. This *Handbook* guides you in taking those skills and applying them in the policy-making arena. Please remember also that the staff of the Department of Public Policy at CEC Headquarters is always available to assist you in your advocacy efforts.

CEC is pleased to share these strategies with you. Please let us know if you identify other advocacy-related strategies that would be helpful to share with those in the education field.

WHAT THIS HANDBOOK CAN DO FOR YOU

The Council for Exceptional Children (CEC) members are instrumental in shaping American special education policy and have been for over 72 years. As the largest professional special education organization in the country that advocates for children, youth, and young adults with exceptionalities, the CEC name carries a great deal of clout in state capitals and in Washington, DC, but our name alone cannot ensure passage of positive and progressive special education policies. Our success has always and will continue to rely on our highly committed and motivated members to press for meaningful special education policies at the grass-roots level.

This handbook will help you channel your drive, strength, commitment, and knowledge of the special education field into effective advocacy efforts. The *Handbook* includes background and technical information to help you implement positive special education policies. It describes the history and evolution of current concerns and explains other successful advocacy efforts upon which you can draw in your own planning.

Although policy making is an erratic process, with the players and politics constantly changing, the basic tools for advocacy never change. These tools, which include knowledge of the legislative or regulatory process, effective communication skills, and accessing the media, are fully discussed in the *Handbook*.

The *Handbook* illuminates what motivates both elected and non-elected officials, what catches their attention, what makes them respond. It demystifies policy making so you understand that influencing the outcome is within your power.

This handbook also helps you organize and prepare for advocating in the interest of students with exceptionalities. It offers advice on building coalitions. It teaches you how to frame the key issues and how to package the important information. And it helps you understand how to use the media as a tool to advance your cause.

Feel free to use sections of this handbook in your own efforts. Where the material suits your needs, copy it directly or change it in any way that helps you apply it to your unique situation.

Most importantly, stay in touch with CEC Headquarters and with your CEC federations/provinces and divisions. Take advantage of the materials others developed, the data on which they relied, and the methods they devised to achieve success. A great way to share your activities with other CEC members is to write an article for our newsletter, *CEC Today*.

Send copies of the printed matter you develop in your campaigns for advocacy to CEC's Department of Public Policy, so they can be incorporated into future advocacy support and training materials. Consider this handbook to be a living document to help us create a more productive and fulfilling nation for students with exceptionalities.

CEC's Department of Public Policy

Telephone 703/264-9498   FAX 703/620-4334

WHAT THIS HANDBOOK CANNOT DO FOR YOU

The reasonable man adapts himself to the world;
the unreasonable man persists in trying to adapt the
world to himself. Therefore, all progress depends on
the unreasonable man.

George Bernard Shaw

Legislative bodies and individual legislators at the state and federal levels all have some things in common and some things that are unique. This handbook offers general information and suggests common approaches. It describes efforts that have succeeded in other places to achieve reform. But no publication can serve as a cookbook for public policy. There will be no precise formula for every situation you will encounter. You should make a long-range plan for change, and within this some short-range goals, and learn all that you can about the policymakers you target. You must, however, stay open-minded and flexible. The system must be ready to respond quickly, even when the unexpected occurs. Most important, you must be prepared to seize every opportunity that presents itself to further your goals.

Effective advocacy is an art. Most of what you will learn about advocacy will come through on-the-job training. While you will discover a lot from reading this handbook, there is no substitute for practice and experience.

Effective advocacy is its own reinforcement. Sometimes you will work very hard and achieve very little. But sometimes, maybe when you least expect it, you will see things change. There are few greater rewards than the feeling that comes from knowing you have made a difference. But remember, you will never know this feeling unless you try.

HOW TO CHANGE PUBLIC POLICY

Social reform can be an arduous process. To succeed, a reformer must be strong, dedicated, persistent, and willing to work hard. But if you are willing to make the investment required, you can make a difference. This is the key to successful advocacy. There is no mystery about it. Victory will come to those who work hard and stay with it.

Try to remember, however, that you are already an accomplished advocate—both at home or in the classroom. As a teacher, you already know how to provide information that can influence someone to agree with your point of view. Therefore, advocating can be easy; you already have the skills developed for successfully implementing reform. You'll just be using those skills in a different arena.

Public policy is based on a simple commodity that is well within your reach—information. The individual who has accurate, useful, well-packaged, meaningful, and hard-hitting information can exercise great power in the policy-making arena.

You already have some of the information that you will need because it comes from your personal experience. You must be willing to share this very personal information with policymakers, so that they can learn what you already know, which they may never have had the opportunity to really understand.

Other information may not be familiar to you, but it is well within your reach. Once you learn where and how to gather the information you need, how to assemble the facts, and how to package and deliver the message, you are more than half of the way there.

Every policy-making body, from legislatures composed of elected officials, to regulatory agencies run by bureaucrats, to large companies managed by boards of directors, has its own process for decision making and policy implementation. As you learn about the process and the people who control the systems you are trying to influence, you will discover what makes advocacy work, where the intervention points are, who controls access and outcome, what and who determines the timing. You must delve into the system, form personal relationships, and become a part of the process to produce change from within.

   Source: *CEC Special Education Advocacy Handbook*, 1995, The Council for Exceptional Children.

Understanding the process, developing good contacts, having good information, and knowing how to use it is what advocacy is all about. This is why the experience you gain and the skills you develop in advocating for reform can be transferred to other activities at other levels. Once you realize that the system is open and accessible, you will appreciate how much power you have as a citizen advocate. If you are willing to work hard and use that power, you can make a big difference.

Source: *CEC Special Education Advocacy Handbook,* 1995, The Council for Exceptional Children.

Stages in Influencing the Policy Process

There are various steps in the policy process—from formulation through implementation—during which you can have a tremendous effect. In order to successfully build your case during any of the steps (e.g., to influence the process), keep the following in mind:

1.) Involve the policymaker in your efforts to effect change.

That way, he or she feels "ownership" towards the issue. For example, say you're collaborating with a regular education teacher in an inclusive classroom and you need more planning time. If you'd like to change your school's policy to ensure that there's a specified amount of time each week for joint planning, problem-solving, and other collaborative activities, involve your principal from the beginning; ask his or her guidance on how to establish a new policy. Or, if the policy change requires an amendment in your state's special education law, contact your state legislator and describe what you feel is the problem to him or her. That way, as the new policy is being developed, any adjustment in the policy's design and procedures can be accomplished with both the knowledge and support of the policymaker.

2.) Make sure your reasons for change are sound.

Often, policymakers attempt to enlist support from other policymakers or from his or her constituents. He or she needs descriptions of individual cases from you that have persuasive potential. But, while such case studies are useful in illustrating a point, policymakers are typically most interested in findings that are based on representative samples and that can be appropriately generalized to the population of interest. For example, if you want to show that it's advantageous to have specified time each week to collaborate and plan classroom activities, provide your principal with specific examples of benefits that result from this type of collaboration.

          Source: *CEC Special Education Advocacy Handbook*, 1995, The Council for Exceptional Children.

3.) The information you provide should be timely and appropriate based on the current stage of policy development.

These stages, which are fairly consistent across federal, state, or local levels, are as follows:

- **Policy enactment**—This includes steps that take place from policy formation through the point at which the policy is actually finalized. The first step is to identify a problem as a policy problem (e.g., a problem that is significant in scope that can be addressed by the enactment or change of a policy). During the next, or formulation step, an effort is made to identify those conditions or procedures that are likely to solve the problem, so that these can be included in the policy. In our previous example of ensuring that teachers in your school have collaboration time each week, a condition of the policy needs to be added which specifies that your pay will not be reduced by the corresponding amount of time spent on collaboration. As the proposed policy is refined, policymakers often turn their attention to how much the new policy will cost, what impact it will have, and how much administrative burden it will require. This would be a good time for you to provide an estimate of both the policy's costs and benefits to the policymaker. In our example, this would also be an appropriate time to provide a copy of "Creating Schools for All Our Students: What 12 Schools Have to Say," (order # P5064) to the policymaker as well. During the third, or deliberation step, your tasks may center around attempts to persuade those with different perspectives to agree with you. You may also need to compromise a few details of the policy during this step in order to rally as many policymakers as you can to your side. The final step is the actual decision or enactment of the policy.

- **Policy implementation**—After your policy is enacted, it must be carried out. It must be incorporated into the ongoing procedures, routines, or activities of your school superintendent, principal, and the teachers in your classroom as well as others that will benefit from specified collaboration time. This is a good time for you to be involved, to offer your school any insight or assistance should any "glitches" in the procedures arise.

- **Policy oversight**—Once a policy is enacted, the policymakers must often review it to make sure the intended effects are being met. For example, is the new policy working? How is it affecting and benefiting students, both with and without disabilities? During this stage, policymakers often identify unmet or emerging needs (e.g., due to the new policy, more teachers are working longer hours in order to accommodate the added collaboration time). Be a resource by sharing tips on how you plan and organize your free time.

4.) Present your information in the most effective way possible.

You need to understand the policymaker and then tailor your "presentation" in a way that will increase the chances of him/her accepting your suggestion and incorporating it into current school policy. For example, if you know that another school in your district tried to have an established "collaboration" time built into their school week, but was viewed as unproductive, refer to the past experiences and suggest changes that will make the program in your school more successful.

- Present your point of view in a clear and concise manner, with details to back you up.

- Present only information that clearly pertains to the policy issue. For example, do not bring up the fact that a particular classroom needs new computers during your explanation of the benefits of collaboration time.

- Present your information in a variety of ways, in order to accommodate various learning styles (e.g., through letters, charts, graphs, or speaking directly with the policymaker).

And finally, since often more than one policymaker is involved in deciding whether a particular policy should be implemented, focus some of your efforts on the policymaker's colleagues, especially those he or she respects or is influenced by.

Source: *CEC Special Education Advocacy Handbook*, 1995, The Council for Exceptional Children.

Myths About Advocacy

Myth: Advocacy is somehow a "dirty" business.

Fact: Advocating social policies—working to correct what is wrong—is your responsibility and your right. Only those who do not understand how public policy is made could believe that citizens should not engage in advocacy. Wanting to leave the world a better place than you found it is admirable. If your cause is worthy, you should feel proud to advocate for it. It is the highest form of participation in an open democracy.

Myth: Advocacy is for professional lobbyists.

Fact: People who have been advocates for a long time have the experience and perspective that can only come with time. Advocates who are well-connected and know their subject matter well can be very valuable to legislators who are pressed for time, who have small or no staffs and few other resources, who have many demands on them, and who often need to get good information they can trust very quickly. These are things that a good professional advocate can provide. However, you, too, can provide good and trustworthy information. And you have valuable assets that professional advocates do not.

Citizen advocates are inherently credible in a way that professional advocates cannot be. When you advocate social reforms it is because you believe they are right, not because someone is paying you to do so. As an educator, part of your everyday duties include influencing the thoughts, knowledge, and opinions of those you come into contact with. You are already adept at formulating, planning, and presenting information—skills that are important to the advocacy process.

You are also a voting constituent, and you represent an organization composed of other voting constituents. This is a fact that politicians never forget. Your elected representatives hold office to serve you and your fellow constituents. They know that if they perform well, voters will keep them in their jobs.

Myth: ***To be successful in advocacy, you have to "know someone."***

Fact: To be good at persuading anyone, you should know certain things about the individual. Fortunately, politicians lead very public lives, and it is easy to learn a great deal about them.

If members of your CEC federation or division already have personal contacts with officeholders, use them. There is nothing wrong with this approach; in fact, it is recommended.

But if you do not already have personal relationships with the officials who will be important in achieving your goals, form them. Politicians like getting to know new people. If you can, arrange a "reception" or a legislative breakfast so your whole organization can meet and get to know your elected officials. Or, invite them to CEC-sponsored events or school-based activities involving students with exceptionalities. Politicians seldom turn down invitations that give them access to large audiences. Or, simply "drop in" the politician's office for an impromptu visit—often a good way to get acquainted!

Source: *CEC Special Education Advocacy Handbook*, 1995, The Council for Exceptional Children.

What Makes Politicians Tick

Politicians have some common characteristics that make the outcome of advocacy efforts more predictable. Knowing these characteristics, and knowing how to take advantage of them, can improve your chances for success.

- **Politicians hold public office to help others.**

    Politicians have chosen to apply their ego strength to public service. Most people run for public office to be in a position to help others. You should remember this when you approach your policymakers because you need the help that they can give.

- **Politicians like to be asked for help.**

    Few politicians come to public office with a preformed personal agenda. Their platforms are usually composed of issues they think are important to their constituents. Few politicians will reach out to correct a social wrong simply because it is there. Rather, they have to be made aware of the problem, be given background information about the problem, be provided with suggestions to solve the problem, and asked for their help in solving it. Get used to the idea that asking for help is a sign of strength, not weakness.

- **Politicians are good learners.**

    By and large, politicians are intelligent. Almost by definition, they have good people skills, "street smarts," and political acumen. In addition, as they serve in public office over time, they learn a great deal. Some of them become experts in particular fields. The best politicians continue to learn throughout life. Remember this when you formulate your plans, because to achieve success, there are important things you should teach policymakers.

- **Politicians do not know everything.**

    Politicians must follow many different issues. Even the most astute and hardworking politician has to deal every day with issues about which he or she knows little or nothing. At the federal level, during an average session (e.g., 1 year of a 2-year Congress), members are asked to cast between 500 and 600 votes. There is no time to become expert in all, or even in most of the areas these votes will cover. Therefore, good politicians are always open to good information. Once they find a reliable source for good information, they will take good care of it and refer to it often.

- **Politicians have many demands on their time.**

  Politicians always have more to do than they can get done. This fact offers several important clues for your approach to them. First, never waste a politician's time. Second, do not overload your elected representative with demands, but work to make his or her job easier. In other words, don't expect to sit back and let the politician work for you. You must help him/her to help you reach your goals. Third, since politicians must prioritize the issues they handle and will inevitably ignore those that fall to the bottom of the list, you must work to frame your issue as important and achievable.

- **Politicians do not have sufficient resources to meet the demands made on them.**

  At the federal level, members of the House and Senate have large staffs and large budgets, but they also have large constituencies to serve. In many states, elected representatives are expected to cover the same broad issues with no staff at all. This is why at the state level, good information, trusted informants, and other outside resources are even more precious. The more you can do for those you ask to represent your issue, the better. If a lasting relationship grows out of your work on special education issues, so much the better.

- **Politicians are always running for office.**

  Elected politicians have two very different jobs: running for office, and making policy while in office. Only one of these is indispensable. The fact that they serve at the will of the people makes politicians very responsive to their constituents. Therefore, try to visit a politician in the company of at least one voting constituent (e.g., a

Source: *CEC Special Education Advocacy Handbook*, 1995, The Council for Exceptional Children.

person from his/her home district). And remember that few politicians turn down access to large audiences of voting constituents.

- **Politicians respond to crises.**

  Because of large demands and small resources, politicians seldom have the luxury of long-range planning. Rather, they respond to emergencies, disasters, and whatever is hot in the news. This phenomenon is sometimes called the 60 Minutes Bill. That is, on Monday mornings, politicians in state legislatures all over the country introduce bills to correct whatever crisis was featured most prominently on the Sunday night CBS show, "60 Minutes." Your job is to portray the situation facing students with exceptionalities as a crisis, but one that *can* be remedied.

- **Politicians behave differently when they know they're being watched.**

  This fact does not make politicians any different from the rest of us. It is included here to remind you of the importance of constant monitoring. This may be accomplished through tracking their voting record and using this in your correspondence to them.

- **Politicians like to be thanked.**

  This also does not differentiate elected officials from the rest of humanity, but it is sometimes too easy to forget. You should always express your gratitude when an official has helped you, even if he/she was unable to achieve the desired result. Thank you's are long remembered.

- **Politicians love good press!**

  They love it when you can make them look good, especially when it's done with little or no effort on their part. Bring your camera and take pictures, then send them to the local press.

Personal Ingredients for Effective Advocacy

Just as it is important to know the objects of your advocacy efforts, it is important to know—and to control—how you are perceived.

The cardinal rule for every encounter with every community leader, politician, and media gatekeeper is to be pleasant. Regardless of how you may differ on important issues, the personal impression you leave will determine whether or not you will be welcomed back. You always want to keep that option open.

Anger is a common reaction to the lack of support involving issues affecting students with exceptionalities. But outward displays of anger are not appropriate in your interaction with policymakers. If you cannot control the anger, cannot channel it into a more positive and productive emotion, you may not be the right person to advocate this particular issue.

Elected officials are used to being accommodated and they expect it. Be willing to show them deference. Even if you do not respect each politician personally, you should respect the office each holds. Belligerence will not only close doors to you, but will typecast your entire organization, and sometimes, even your cause.

Be honest and straightforward. Because information is the commodity you trade, credibility is absolutely essential to your success. Avoid half-truths that have even a chance of being misleading. If you lead politicians down a path where they get ambushed, they will never deal with you again. Remember Mark Twain's advice: "If you tell the truth, you don't have to remember anything."

Persistence is important in successful advocacy, but beware of crossing the thin line and becoming a pest. Basic courtesy should guide your actions. Be sensitive to the many different demands that are made on political leaders, and plan your advocacy efforts accordingly. Be as timely as possible in contacting them about an issue or in providing the necessary information.

Source: *CEC Special Education Advocacy Handbook*, 1995, The Council for Exceptional Children.

Rules For Effective Advocacy

Most of what a good advocate does is intuitive and grows out of a few basic principles. Following is the core set of principles on which most advocates agree.

Try to remember these principles when you become discouraged, entangled in detail, or simply confused. They may help clear your head, renew, and redirect your energies.

1.) Ask for what you want.

For a variety of reasons, many of us hesitate to ask for what we really want. There is no place for such hesitation in advocating for issues regarding children with exceptionalities. If you do not ask, you will never get the results you seek. Do not be so pushy that you alienate people, but have the "gumption" to ask for what you need.

You can get ideas of what to ask for from many CEC-related resources: your local or state Political Action Network (PAN) Coordinator; information to PAN from CEC's Department of Public Policy (DPP), such as *PAN Alerts* and PAN-O-GRAMS; or by asking a member of DPP what the "hot" issues are.

2.) Be specific in your request.

Generalities won't get you what you want. The more specific you can make your request, the better. State the issue clearly, but briefly. Explain the resolution you seek and describe the impact that will occur if the change being requested is not made.

3.) Be ready to work hard.

There is nothing magical about success in advocacy or success in politics. Victory most often goes to the one who works the hardest. As we will discuss later, coalitions can legitimize your efforts and provide a broad base of support. But there is no substitute for a small team of hardy advocates willing to invest the time and energy necessary to change public policy.

4.) Find a legislative champion.

Advocacy for any special interest breaks down into two parts: advocacy from the inside and advocacy from the outside. CEC staff and members can plan, coordinate, and implement the outside advocacy activities, but only a member of the "club" can handle the inside responsibilities.

One of the first things you must do is find a legislative champion who is willing to take up your cause with his or her colleagues. This special person should be:

- **ideally, in a leadership position or holding a seat on a key committee; if possible, a committee that has responsibility for disability/gifted issues;**

- **at a minimum, well-liked by his or her peers;**

- **committed to the outcome you seek;**

- **willing to work your issue; not just vote right, but to really work the bill with fellow legislators.**

Begin the search for this special person among the personal contacts and acquaintances of CEC members. Is there someone in the legislature who has a family member with a disability, or a background in working with persons with exceptionalities? Is there someone with whom CEC already has a good relationship? Someone who has championed CEC issues in the past?

If your search does not turn up the ideal inside advocate, you may have to begin a relationship that will create one. Start with members of the legislative subcommittees that will be key to success, such as the Senate Subcommittee on Disability Policy, and the House Subcommittee on Select Education and Civil Rights.* (Call DPP for a list of the members of these subcommittees.) Remember that the issue of exceptional children carries liabilities. Hopefully, you will find a special supporter with similar beliefs, but he/she must also be ready to stand up to stiff competition.

---

* These may change in the 104th Congress. At the time this *Handbook* was printed, the new structure was not yet known. Please call DPP for updates.

Source: *CEC Special Education Advocacy Handbook*, 1995, The Council for Exceptional Children.

Once you have found your champion, have established a good working relationship with him/her and know you can trust him/her, follow his/her lead.

5.) Organize, coordinate, orchestrate.

Plan as much as you can and leave as little as possible to chance. Once the legislative session starts, things can move very quickly, so coordinate carefully with your own troops, the members of your coalition, your legislative champion, and other key members and staff. Work to ensure that all your allies speak with one voice. Reaching a consensus is important. (The time for thrashing out differences is before you approach the legislature.) Remember that elected representatives are most responsive to their own constituents, so always include voting constituents, preferably powerful and politically active ones, on your team.

6.) Touch all the bases.

Talk with and solicit help from as many groups representing the interests of children with exceptionalities as you can. Approach everyone with a vested interest in your issue. Since you will be advocating on a shoestring, do not waste time or effort trying to hide your plans from groups or individuals you think might oppose your efforts. To the contrary, you may find good allies in unlikely places. At the least, you might be able to neutralize some potential opposition. You will also learn what opposition is out there and be in a better position to deal with their objections.

7.) Stay flexible, be opportunistic.

Long-range plans can provide good general guidelines for your advocacy efforts, but it is critical that you remain flexible and willing to fight. Remember that campaigns for advocating rights of children and youth with exceptionalities are like electricity: They do not exist without resistance. You must be ready and able to move quickly, to respond to your opponents, and to take advantage of opportunities to advance your cause as they arise.

8.) Keep it simple.

Policymakers are almost always pressed for time, so it is a serious mistake to waste their time. You should be prepared to state your best case for the issues at hand in 30 seconds. You will have opportunities to discuss the issues in greater depth, but you should always strive to capture your audience's attention within the first few sentences. Always plan your presentations as if your audience will only remember one line from everything that you say. Decide ahead of time what that one line should be (think of it as the headline), and design your message around it. Keep your message simple, appealing, brief, and to the point. Avoid abbreviations and special education jargon.

Any written documents that you leave behind should be concise and to the point (chart and table formats work well). Material that fits onto one page has the best chance of being read. Attach backup and supporting information as appendices (but even the appendices need to be brief, organized, and clear as to what they reference and support). When a legislator or a staff person wants more information, you can always supply it. But unsolicited lengthy documents have slim chances of ever getting read.

9.) Assume the perspective of others.

Remember that policymakers hold positions of power. They are used to having a great deal of control over their surroundings and consequently, they often do not easily understand the difficulties children and youth with exceptionalities face.

Be patient and understanding in your approach to policymakers. Listen to the questions they ask for clues about their thinking. Remember that once you, too, knew very little about the issues regarding children and youth with exceptionalities. Work to fit what you have learned through personal experience into the framework of persons who have never had those experiences.

Source: *CEC Special Education Advocacy Handbook*, 1995, The Council for Exceptional Children.

10.) Build and preserve your credibility.

This admonition means more than simply never telling a lie. It means that you should keep your legislative champion and your other allies fully informed, especially about the political climate that surrounds your proposed legislation. You should not mislead allies. Do not promise more than you can deliver. And, do not spring any surprises.

11.) Anticipate and deal with your opposition.

People who oppose you may approach the issue from a different perspective, and they represent people with different interests. Do not take the differences between you personally, but do not ignore them either. See them as the challenge they are. Plan for opposition to your advocacy efforts and design ways to deal with it.

Use the contacts and personal connections you have to neutralize as much opposition as you can. Even where an organization formally opposes your goal, they might be willing to hold their active advocacy against it in check. But do not rely on a promise of passivity, and be prepared to deal with antagonism. Have your own facts and figures ready. Work constantly to portray your bill not as another break for children and youth with exceptionalities, but as a civil rights issue, economic issue, etc.

12.) Be prepared to compromise.

Because public policy balances competing interests, flexibility is essential. You should be prepared to negotiate, and have a fall-back position. Avoid show-downs. You run the risk of losing your credibility.

Remember that social policy is an evolutionary process. Change often comes in small increments. If you do not get all that you seek the first time you ask (and you probably will not), try to ensure that the work you do constructs a base on which you can build your future efforts. Sometimes it is advantageous to have a long-range plan with several short-range alternatives.

13.) Never burn your bridges.

Avoid making enemies in your advocacy efforts. Alliances shift in the public policy arena, and opponents on one issue become allies on another. Deal with your adversaries as you would like them to deal with you. Remember, in advocacy, there are no permanent friends and no permanent enemies.

14.) Target your efforts.

Trying to persuade every single member of the legislature on your issue would be exhausting and wasteful. Some members will almost always support you, and others will almost always oppose you. Focus your efforts on the key players (the leadership, relevant committee members, and those with recognized expertise on special education issues), and the swing votes (those who begin on the fence but whom advocacy might move to your side). Do not forget your supporters. They need effort, just not as much.

15.) Honor the staff.

Do not underestimate the importance of staff in a policy-making body. The members for whom they work trust and defer to them; you should, too. Do not necessarily insist on speaking with the legislator personally; it is often more advantageous to speak with the staffers. Because they are free from political demands, including campaigning, staff often develop greater substantive expertise than their bosses. If they want to, they can be a tremendous help. Treat staff well. They also like to be thanked and kept well-informed.

16.) Track your progress.

Keep flow charts and checklists to monitor your progress. Once the legislative session starts, you will be racing the clock, so do not let the pace make you lose track of your issue. Avoid making a pest of yourself, but check in with your supporters often to make sure their position does not change. (Your opposition will be checking in with them.) Keep a careful count of the votes you have and the votes you need. Watch the deadlines.

  Source: *CEC Special Education Advocacy Handbook*, 1995, The Council for Exceptional Children.

Do not force a wavering member into the opponent's camp by trying too hard to pin the person down. Learn how to accurately interpret statements that appear supportive on the surface but do not constitute a commitment (e.g., "I'd like to be with you on this one" or "I think you have a good case here"). Also, try not to let a legislator commit him/herself to the opposition's position.

17.) Be persistent.

Few important social reforms are achieved the first time they are sought, so do not be discouraged by failure. Sometimes sheer persistence is what wins in the end because each time a member turns you down, he/she feels more like he/she owes you in the future.

18.) Follow up.

Learn as you go by taking the time after the dust settles to ask questions. Debrief your allies to reinforce your strengths and shore up your weaknesses. Advocacy is an art form learned on the job, so work to get better at it as you go along.

If you have worked as a group, members of the group need to share responses, activities, feelings, etc. This information can be used to plan strategies for the next time.

Always remember to thank your supporters. It is not only the decent thing to do, but it will make them more willing to help in the future.

THE CREATION, CARE, AND FEEDING OF COALITIONS

There are many ways you can advocate for special education as an individual. But your impact is multiplied when you join others.

A coalition is a union of people or organizations seeking similar ends. It presents a visible source of information and power and a unified voice to prevent the fragmentation of forces that share common goals. It also prevents governmental bodies from pitting one person/group against another.

Coalitions are delicate. They can be as fragile as a family and require the same loving care. At their heart is the willingness and ability to put aside individual differences for the sake of common goals.

Coalitions can create strength by uniting unlikely allies and bringing unexpected resources to your campaign. When large organizations with established reputations lend their stability and respect to a coalition, it allows the advocacy groups who are the backbone of the coalition to leverage their resources.

Coalition-building should be an important prelude to your campaign for bettering the situation of children and youth with exceptionalities. Remember that coalitions do not just happen. They require planning, persuasion, and constant communication. Natural organizational alliances will differ from one community to another and will shift from issue to issue. As noted before, there are no permanent friends and no permanent enemies in advocacy.

     Source: *CEC Special Education Advocacy Handbook*, 1995, The Council for Exceptional Children.

Networks

Networks are a precursor to coalitions, but they can perform important functions much better than coalitions, because each network participant speaks and acts for him/herself. At its simplest, a student with exceptionalities advocacy network is nothing more than the commitment, communication, and cooperation of individuals who share a dedication to the fair treatment of children and youth with exceptionalities.

Networks have no formal leadership structure. Rather, they are led by those individuals who have the energy, dedication, and skills to reach out to others.

The best network members have most of the following characteristics:

- **a sense of personal mission that drives them (almost always related to a desire to leave the world a better place than it was found);**

- **a low threshold for inappropriate outrage;**

- **a willingness to take calculated risks;**

- **integrity and trustworthiness;**

- **the persistence of a long-distance runner;**

- **a good sense of humor;**

- **a capacity for seeing things not as they are, but as they should be;**

- **spontaneity, flexibility, and adaptability;**

- **raw energy and the capacity to harness the energy of others.**

Successful networks operate at a high level of trust and reciprocity. They rely on a process of faithful exchange which builds and strengthens the more it is used.

Source: *CEC Special Education Advocacy Handbook*, 1995, The Council for Exceptional Children.

Networks excel at developing and introducing new ideas. They perform best those tasks that require individual initiative, quick response, flexibility, risk-taking, and moral intensity.

In forming your students with exceptionalities advocacy network you should draw on your long-standing relationships and personal contacts, but you should also think expansively and creatively. CEC members are familiar with working with groups that serve the special education community. But there may be less obvious groups to tap as allies that would give more strength to the network by making the issue more pervasive (e.g., regular education organizations, local businesses, teachers unions, social service agencies, parent groups, chapters/branches of the National Association for the Education of Young Children, etc.).

There are many places where you might find new allies on special education-related issues.

All communities have leaders who affect public policy because they are powerful, well-liked, or both. Sometimes these leaders take a visible public role. But other leaders are just as influential in a much less obvious way. Advocates who really know their communities will know how to find even these more obscure individuals.

You should try to "round up" the key players for their active participation in your campaign, but do not be concerned if they refuse. They might be willing to support your effort at a lower level or at a later date. The least you will have accomplished is advising them of your intentions and your goals, and hopefully, neutralizing any opposition they might have otherwise posed. In the end, the core members of your students with exceptionalities advocacy network, the real activists, will emerge naturally through their hard work and commitment.

Source: *CEC Special Education Advocacy Handbook*, 1995, The Council for Exceptional Children.

Building Coalitions

Coalitions are alliances of organizations working together toward a common goal. Coalitions can be formal or informal, tightly or loosely organized. They can be temporary, created for only a limited purpose (such as marshalling support for a specific vote), or they can be permanent, dedicated to long-term, comprehensive reform.

While networks tend to be decentralized, coalitions are centralized and hierarchical. This is because the participants in a network speak only for themselves, but the participants in a coalition represent entire organizations.

In contrast to networks, coalitions provide organizational structure, institutional resources, visibility, and respectability. Like networks, except in a larger and less intense way, coalitions harness and focus the energies of their constituents and multiply their effectiveness in seeking social change.

The great strength of coalitions is their diversity. Some angles of special education issues may appeal more to one group than to another, but in general, it is better to frame the issue for broader, rather than narrower, appeal. However, including uncooperative groups in a coalition can be destructive. Successful coalitions are composed of members who are willing to put aside their own egos, and the conflicting needs of their individual organizations, for the common ultimate goal.

At the same time, a successful coalition respects the needs of its individual member organizations. Each organization should remain free to act and speak for itself outside of the coalition. No one should speak formally for the coalition on issues or positions that have not been cleared and agreed upon. But a successful coalition must have a management and decision-making structure that permits prompt, flexible, and conclusive action.

Begin your coalition by forming an organizing committee to develop a detailed statement of principles and goals. Have members of the organizing committee recruit organizations. Plan a program for the coalition based on incremental steps—e.g., build in ways for your members to experience success. Focus clearly on a single target mission; don't scatter and spread yourselves too thin.

If you feel comfortable doing so, and if the formation of your coalition constitutes a news event, you can hold a joint press conference. This presents the opportunity to:

- **Publicly commit participating organizations—including their members and staff—to the coalition;**

- **Bring media attention that will convey the coalition's purpose and commitment;**

- **Recruit other individuals and organizations.**

Source: *CEC Special Education Advocacy Handbook*, 1995, The Council for Exceptional Children.

FRAMING THE ISSUES

One of the most important precepts for success in both political and media advocacy is to understand and appreciate your audience. Regardless of how good your intentions are, regardless of how sure you are about the message you want to send, the only thing that really counts is the message that is received. If all your work fails to take account of the background and experience of your audience, and the context in which your message is heard, it could be for naught.

We are all bombarded with information. This is even more true for policymakers. It is literally impossible to pay attention to all the information that surrounds us; we filter and sift this information, and that protects us from becoming overwhelmed. But the filtering process can also prevent important information from getting through. No amount of effort can make a message work if it doesn't get through to people.

Designing your message to get through the audience's mental filters is critical. So, too, is dealing with the information that already exists in the listener's mind. Information is never received in a vacuum. Rather, it enters and resonates (or competes) with an existing body of knowledge and experience. In developing your advocacy message, you should not begin with what it is that you want to say. Rather, you should begin by knowing what is already there. Then frame your message to take advantage of the existing knowledge. Framing means putting your information into a context. For example, if you're advocating for increased special education funding for your state, you might want to relay some "success" stories of students who benefited from a special education program in your legislator's district. When done well, framing makes bare facts come alive. It personalizes abstract ideas and illuminates their relevance and importance.

Everyone holds certain convictions and beliefs that can be evoked by your message. Though we are a very heterogeneous nation, Americans resonate with surprising unanimity to a set of core public values: freedom, security, family, fairness, opportunity, and caring. When your message evokes these values, your audience is not only more receptive to the content of what you say, they actually become involved in it.

Source: *CEC Special Education Advocacy Handbook*, 1995, The Council for Exceptional Children.

27

Resonating with your audience, or striking a responsive chord with existing values and beliefs, changes your audience from passive recipients of information to active participants in communication. This co-creative process is the highest level of persuasion. It gives your message high impact and leaves your audience feeling involved.

Because of the electronic media, we live in the age of the 9-second media bite. This is not necessarily bad, it is simply a fact of modern life. It suggests that you should design your message to be short and to the point. Work hard to translate what you want to say into simple concepts that can evoke strong emotions. For example, if your goal is to establish a procedure for mediation in your state/province, instead of complaining repeatedly about the current system, *concisely* state what the positive benefits of such a process could be (e.g., financial, time-saving, beneficial to both schools and parents, etc.). Many people would respond more positively to your constructive ideas than to your complaints.

As applied to politicians, these principles require you to learn as much as you can about their current beliefs and attitudes toward children and youth with exceptionalities.

Source: *CEC Special Education Advocacy Handbook*, 1995, The Council for Exceptional Children.

UNDERSTANDING THE LEGISLATIVE PROCESS

To be good at advocating your state legislators and the Congress, you should understand the rules under which they work. This is not difficult, because once you get past a little technical vocabulary and the customs based largely in parliamentary procedure, the legislative system makes sense. Learning how the process works is easy because many people are interested in it, and hence, there are many sources of information and help.

Each state legislature will have its own particular rules, staffing system, committee structure, and calendar. But they all have a lot in common with each other and with the United States Congress. What follows is an outline of the federal system for your background information. To learn the particulars in your own state, contact your federation Political Action Network (PAN) Coordinator. If you're not sure who your state/province PAN Coordinator is, contact CEC's Department of Public Policy at 703/264-9498.

Source: *CEC Special Education Advocacy Handbook*, 1995, The Council for Exceptional Children.

How a Federal Bill Becomes a Law

Most bills are introduced because of constituent interest. Very few bills are introduced that will not be popular with at least one constituent group. Largely to keep constituents happy, many more bills are introduced each session than ever become law.

Laws begin with a good idea. The idea is then translated into technical language by a legislative drafter. Any Member of either chamber (the U.S. House of Representatives or the U.S. Senate) can introduce a bill. In the House, it is referred to as "dropping it into the hopper" (literally, the name of the box into which bills are dropped).

The bill is assigned a number, prefixed with "H.R." in the House and "S." in the Senate. When it is printed, it will also carry the names of the original sponsors, although additional Members may sign on as sponsors at any time.

The bill is then referred to the appropriate committee(s). This referral is technically considered the "first reading." It is in the committee structure that the substance of the bill comes under closest scrutiny and where the large majority of bills die.

If a bill's chances for passage are considered good, a frequent next step is a request for comment by interested government agencies. The committee chairman may assign the bill to a subcommittee, or it may be considered by the full committee. Hearings may be held on the bill; they can be open to the public, closed, or both.

After hearings and a vote, the subcommittee can sit on the bill or refer it back to the full committee with recommendations for action and for any amendments. This is called "ordering a bill reported." The full committee can then "mark up" or make amendments and vote on the measure. Or it can "kill" it through inaction. If reported back to the full House or Senate, the bill will be put on a calendar that will affect how and when it will receive further consideration.

In the House, the Rules Committee controls the flow of legislation by issuing rules for floor debate. There are technical ways to end-run the Rules Committee, but the Committee exercises considerable power. It will decide whether amendments will be entertained (debate under an "open rule") or not ("closed rule"). The length for debate in the House

Source: *CEC Special Education Advocacy Handbook*, 1995, The Council for Exceptional Children.

varies, but is always limited. Debate in the Senate is usually unlimited, although a filibuster can be halted by a three-fifths majority vote on "cloture."

A bill can be voted on many times, not just in subcommittee and full committee, but often on the rule for it and usually on any amendments considered on the floor of the full chamber. Amendments can even be amended. After amendments have been voted on, a motion may be made to recommit the bill to committee (this does not happen very often). If a bill survives this motion, it is "read for the third time," and a vote is taken on final passage. In the full Senate, a vote can be by voice (uncounted), by standing (counted but not recorded), or by recorded roll call. In the House, recorded votes are done electronically.

If passed in one chamber, the bill is sent to the other. There it can be passed as is, sent to committee, rejected, ignored, or passed with substitute language. If the opposite chamber alters the bill submitted to it, the differing versions from each house are "sent to conference." There, conferees from both chambers try to work out the differences between them through compromise. This can be a long, drawn-out process, and sometimes bills die in conference. However, when agreement is reached, a conference report is prepared that embodies the compromises, and the conference report is voted on by each body. Approval of the report constitutes approval of the compromise bill. A bill may also move concurrently through the House and Senate.

After the same bill has been passed by both chambers, it is sent to the President. He can sign it, thereby enacting it into law immediately. If he does not sign it and Congress is in session, it becomes law automatically after 10 days. If he does not sign it and Congress is not in session, it dies after 10 days (this is known as a "pocket veto"). He can also veto it by returning it to Congress within 10 days with a message stating his reasons. A recorded two-thirds vote of all present (and they must equal at least a quorum) in both houses is required to override a veto. Otherwise the measure is killed.

It is obvious why it is so much easier to kill a bill than to pass one. The rules that govern Congress can be changed, but most of the time they operate to keep the pace of legislation slow and deliberative.

A Typical Journey for Legislation in Congress

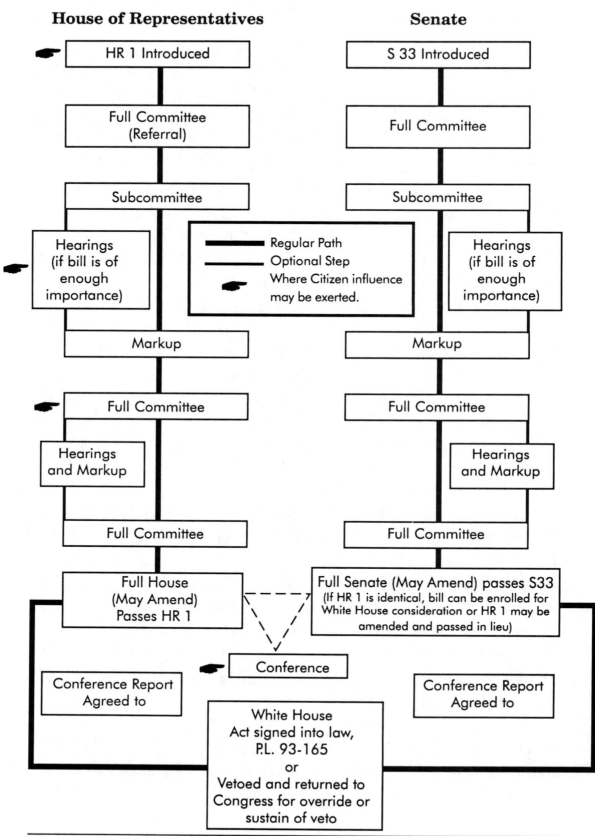

  Source: *CEC Special Education Advocacy Handbook*, 1995, The Council for Exceptional Children.

Steps for Success

Do not become mired in the details of the legislative process. It is more important that you prepare your materials, organize your coalition, and locate and enlist the commitment of your legislative champion. These are the things that only you can do. The members who support your issue and their staffs will help with the legislative details.

You should carefully monitor the many different places your bill could die. You may also have to serve as the bridge between the two legislative chambers, where your tactics may radically differ. In some states, each house is under the control of a different party. Even when controlled by the same party, communication between them may be sparse. Often some of the best information a good advocate can offer is about the other chamber's activities.

Meet with or call your legislative champion frequently to find out what he or she needs you to do. Arrange for as many other members as possible to be contacted by their constituents—in person, by letter, or by phone—in support of your measure.

Identify and target key committee members and important swing votes. Organize small advocacy teams—no more than three or four carefully selected persons who come from the particular member's district, who are known by him or her, or who will be considered to be important—to meet and work these key members.

Prepare packets of one-page fact sheets and background materials that you can leave behind. These materials should introduce and explain your organization network and/or your coalition. They should lay out the facts about children and youth with exceptionalities and the arguments for the specific issues you are addressing.

Keep track of your bill's progress through the system. Timing is very important. Debrief your troops constantly. Remember that things happen quickly during short legislative sessions. Keep a running tally of your supporters and opponents so that you can direct your efforts most efficiently.

Always keep your eye on the opponents of your bill. While you work for passage of your own bill, you may have to oppose rival legislation that would negate your efforts or cause confusion when implementation occurs.

Source: *CEC Special Education Advocacy Handbook,* 1995, The Council for Exceptional Children.

33

Legislative Hearings

You should work hard to get legislative hearings scheduled for your bill as it winds its way through the committee structure. Hearings are sometimes even held on issues for which there is no pending legislation, though this is less common.

Hearings function to create a public record. They are almost always tightly controlled and well orchestrated; seldom are any surprises sprung at a hearing. Nevertheless, they are often attended by the press, and they present an excellent opportunity to advocate your position, both directly to the key policymakers and indirectly through the media. Hearings also serve as an important rallying point and reinforcement for your hardworking supporters.

A legislator who supports your cause must arrange the hearing. Working with him or her, you should plan the hearing to demonstrate as broad a base to your support as you can muster. Draw on your students with exceptionalities advocacy network and coalition, and your broader CEC contacts. Look to your local or state universities for experts in special education who might lay out the issue from a medical, research, or scientific point of view. If you cannot get these key individuals to testify, see if they will submit short written statements for the record in support of your bill, or at least letters of support.

If you have never seen a hearing, try to attend one that is held before the same committee as will hold yours.

Work hard to prepare your supporting witnesses for their testimony. Help them frame their message in terms most supportive of your position. Unless they are seasoned veterans of legislative hearings, rehearse their testimony with them, and practice a question and answer dialog like the one in which they might become engaged with members of the committee.

It is sometimes difficult for academics to avoid technical language. Help your witnesses understand that committee members may have very little knowledge of special education and might be put off by jargon. Witnesses must also show deference and never speak down to elected officials. Witnesses should use clear, direct, and simple language that,

   Source: *CEC Special Education Advocacy Handbook*, 1995, The Council for Exceptional Children.

if picked up directly by the press, could convey their message to a broad general audience.

At the hearing, witnesses will probably be asked to limit their oral testimony to 5 to 7 minutes. This is a request you must honor. Your written testimony, which should be prepared in multiple copies for distribution to members of the committee and the press, can be longer than what was presented verbally and can include much of the background and supporting information that you will not have a chance to present orally.

For highest impact, your oral statement should not be simply a reading of your written statement. In fact, your oral statement should not be read at all, but delivered from the heart, directly to the committee members as if they were guests in your home.

You want the committee members to get to know you and your CEC organization during this hearing.

Speak from experience in the same way you would in a conversation with a friend. You want these members to fully understand issues related to children and youth with exceptionalities and to feel eager to correct the current wrongs.

The only exceptions to time limitations on oral statements are if members of the committee ask you questions and engage you in a dialogue. This is exactly what you want to happen. It might reveal misunderstandings they have and give you the opportunity to correct them. It can increase the members' involvement with, and hence commitment to, your issue. And it will build a longer record. Remember, if these members like you, your organization, and your coalition, they will want to work more with you in the future.

Do not feel compelled to answer any question that you do not think is proper or on point. If an irrelevant question is asked, try to steer the conversation back on course with a polite rephrasing in order to address the issue at hand. Also, never be embarrassed if you are asked a question to which you do not know the answer. Rather, offer to get the information the questioner seeks and submit it for the record. Then be sure to follow through.

Begin with your main point and stay with it. If opponents of your bill have testified before you, use your testimony to rebut their most damaging points. If they will not testify until later, anticipate and deal with their opposition.

When You Testify Before a Legislative Body

From time to time, you may be called upon to testify and/or write testimony. The purpose of testifying before a congressional committee, subcommittee, or state legislative committee is to present the views of CEC, its divisions, and other units to the elected officials concerned with new legislation or in developing amendments to current laws. Testimony may also be given at state or federal advisory committees. Before preparing testimony, it is important to consult with others involved in the topic under consideration, as well as be familiar with existing position papers and reference material.

Whenever you testify before a legislative body, always address the chair of the committee first, and then the committee members themselves. This applies each and every time you respond to a question from the panel, whether or not the chairman asks it himself.

Identifying Testifiers

Because the need to testify may come up with limited advance notice (sometimes as little as 7 days), it is important to have a list of persons who would be willing and able to prepare and give testimony. In some cases, the testimony may be written by one individual or committee/ group but presented by someone else.

     Source: *CEC Special Education Advocacy Handbook*, 1995, The Council for Exceptional Children.

Tips for Testimony

The following tips should be reviewed for usage when preparing and testifying before legislative or advisory committees.

1. Identify yourself, and, if applicable, the organization you represent.

2. State your position for or against the proposed bill or action.

3. Summarize your recommendations first and then add explanation.

    Include answers to the following questions.

    a. What is your special interest? If testifying as an individual, explain why the proposed bill or administrative rules or action by a governing body would affect the students you serve. If representing a group, explain the group's interest and how you know other members of the group share the opinions expressed in your testimony.

    b. How did you arrive at your conclusions?

    c. Who will benefit or who will be hurt?

        Include the following information:

        I.   Outline of the problem(s) as you see them.

        II. Solutions you think would be acceptable and alternatives to proposed solutions with which you do not agree.

        III. The positive aspects of the issue.

        IV. Statistics, charts, and graphs when relevant.

        V.   In general, testimony should be brief (around 5-7 minutes), stimulating, and overstated in order to excite and energize the legislators about needed programs or changes.

Source: *CEC Special Education Advocacy Handbook*, 1995, The Council for Exceptional Children.

VI.   Avoid attacking other groups, organizations, individuals, or other educational agendas. This could backfire and have the reverse effect and lower your credibility.

4.   Sum up your position at the end.

5.   Have enough copies of your testimony available to give to each legislator and to the press.

6.   Avoid: cliches (e.g., "It takes a whole village to raise a child,"), excessive wordiness, vague generalities, flattery.

7.   Be clear, concise, and brief. Include examples if relevant. If pertinent, explain how present laws or procedures would be negatively affected by proposed bill or procedures.

8.   By all means, use plain English and stay away from jargon used in our field. If you must use a word or phrase that is uncommon, be sure to explain it.

To help understand the art of testimony, it is suggested that you attend at least one hearing at any level of government and review the written testimony given by others. This should better prepare you for the time when you will be called upon.

Source: *CEC Special Education Advocacy Handbook*, 1995, The Council for Exceptional Children.

Letter Writing

A personal letter is an effective way to contact legislators or public officials. Legislators and public officials are very attentive to the views of their constituents. They keep track of the number of letters received on any given issue. Following are a few guidelines to help you write an effective letter to your state legislator or public official:

Address your letter properly with your legislator's or public official's full name and correct spelling. Suggested addresses and salutations:

The Honorable (full name)
U.S. Senate
Washington, DC 20510

Dear Senator (last name):

The Honorable (full name)
U.S. House of Representatives
Washington, DC 20515

Dear Representative (last name):

The Honorable (full name)
Governor
State Capital
City, State, Zip

Dear Governor (full name):

Source: *CEC Special Education Advocacy Handbook*, 1995, The Council for Exceptional Children.

The Honorable (full name)
State Senator
State Capital
City, State, Zip

Dear Senator (last name):

The Honorable (full name)
State Representative
State Capital
City, State, Zip

Dear Representative (last name):

Source: *CEC Special Education Advocacy Handbook,* 1995, The Council for Exceptional Children.

Tips On Writing To Legislators And Public Officials

- Do not use form letters.

- A typed letter is not always preferable. However, make sure your letter is legible.

- Use a complete return address on the envelope and in the letter.

- Keep letters short and concise.

- Identify your subject clearly in the first paragraph: include the bill number(s) and legislation.

- Use titles, if appropriate (e.g., Dear Senator ____).

- Give reasons for your position. If you have specialized knowledge, share it with your legislator.

- Be constructive, not negative. Admit that problems exist and suggest practical alternatives.

- Request a reply from your legislator outlining his/her views and intended action.

- Keep letters to one subject/issue to avoid confusion.

- Be reasonable. Do not ask for the impossible.

- Do not assume that your legislator knows as much as you do on a particular subject.

- Write your letter when the bill is in committee or subcommittee or when you receive a call for action from CEC Headquarters, your Federation office, or your PAN Coordinator.

- Avoid stereotyped phrases and sentences that give the appearance of a form letter.

- Letters from personal friends of the legislator often receive priority. Use board members and other contacts effectively.

- Sign your letter over your typed name, if appropriate.

- Remember to write a letter of appreciation when you feel your legislator has done a good job, or when he/she has been particularly responsive to concerns you have expressed.

- Send a copy of your letter and response to the Department of Public Policy at CEC Headquarters and to your PAN Coordinator.

Sample Letters

Personal Opinion Message

Senator (NAME)
Washington, DC (ZIP)

The _____ Council
for Exceptional Children urges
your support for Harkin Amendment to Labor, HHS, Appropriations Bill for special education.

Sam Smith
PAN Coordinator

Mailgram

DATE

Representative (NAME)
Washington, DC (ZIP)

Dear Representative:
The Council for Exceptional Children
applauds you for the concern that you
are demonstrating in seeking increased
fiscal support for preschool programs for
children with disabilities. Evidence demonstrates that with early intervention
some disabling conditions are reversible,
some conditions can be ameliorated, and
the multiplying consequences of a disability can be curtailed.

(Sign your name, title, affiliation)

Source: *CEC Special Education Advocacy Handbook*, 1995, The Council for Exceptional Children.

April 12, 1993

The Honorable Major Owens
United States House of Representatives
2305 Rayburn House Office Building
Washington, DC 20515

Dear Representative Owens:

On behalf of the 54,000 members of The Council for Exceptional Children, I would like to express our deep appreciation for your inspirational keynote address at the 1993 Council for Exceptional Children Convention. Having someone of your stature, as the Chairman of the Subcommittee on Select Education, speak to the needs of children with exceptionalities greatly contributed to the overwhelming success of our convention.

I personally want to thank you for your remarks concerning special education during the keynote address. Your comments on the national debate on the inclusion of children with disabilities in regular classrooms set the stage for the CEC Delegate Assembly's adoption of a responsible and child-focused inclusion policy statement. Like you, CEC is concerned that during these tight fiscal times funding for special education will become increasingly vulnerable. It is imperative that we educate our children on the basis of their needs and not on budgetary factors. Furthermore, the federal government must make special education a national priority and live up to the promise made in P.L. 94-142 to fund 40 percent of the national average per pupil expenditure for the education of children with disabilities. By bringing these issues to the forefront in your address, you were able to successfully highlight our concerns on the national stage.

We look forward to working with you during the 103rd Congress. With the reauthorization of the Technology Related Assistance Act approaching, we are certain that your work on behalf of our children will continue. Again, thank you for your sincere and motivational address. We were honored by your presence and your deep commitment to children with exceptionalities.

Sincerely,

Nancy Safer
Interim Executive Director

June 11, 1993

The Honorable Mark O. Hatfield
U.S. Senate
711 Senate Hart Office Building
Washington, DC 20510

Dear Senator Hatfield:

On behalf of The Council for Exceptional Children, an organization of over 54,000 educators, researchers, parents, and others who advocate on behalf of children with disabilities and gifted children, I am writing to convey our strong support of the National Education Goal for Parental Participation Act.

A national education goal for parental participation would serve to stress the need for the involvement of parents in their children's education. A child's first and most important teachers are her or his parents. Schools must strive to involve parents in meaningful and effective ways to ensure the success of a child's comprehensive education. Only parents can create a home environment that will work to sustain and supplement the education received in the classroom. Through a mutually supportive partnership, parents and school professionals can work together to ensure children have the opportunity to reach their individual education goals.

CEC commends you for your foresight in sponsoring this important legislation. The National Education Goals are incomplete without a goal focusing on the need for parental involvement in our neighborhood schools. Thank you for sponsoring the National Education Goal for Parental Participation Act.

Sincerely,

Nancy Safer
Interim Executive Director

Source: *CEC Special Education Advocacy Handbook*, 1995, The Council for Exceptional Children.

June 14, 1993

U.S. Senate
Washington, DC 20510

Dear Senator:

On behalf of The Council for Exceptional Children, an organization of over 54,000 educators, researchers, parents, and others who advocate on behalf of children with disabilities and gifted children, I urge you to support H.R. 2118, the FY 1993 supplemental appropriations bill that will be offered on the Senate floor this week.

The Senate Appropriations Committee has reported a FY 1993 supplemental bill that, unlike the House version, does not terminate education programs. The House bill eliminates 14 education programs for a total education cut of $136 million. The cuts would affect programs such as the Student Literacy Corps, Library Literacy Programs, Bilingual Vocational Training, and State Student Incentive Grants. These programs would be terminated to help pay for summer job initiatives and other programs.

The members of the Senate Appropriations Committee have responsibly decided that it does not make sense to cut education programs in order to fund summer job initiatives. We ask you to support the Committee and vote for the Senate FY 1993 supplemental appropriations bill.

Sincerely,

Joseph Ballard
Director of Governmental Relations

Telephone Calls

- To find out who your Senators or your own member of the House are, call the Capitol Switchboard at 202/224-3121, or the Council of State Governments at 202/624-5460.

- If timeliness is critical, don't write—telephone.

  Do not expect to be put through to your legislator when you call. They cannot talk to every constituent. The staff is there for the purpose of listening to constituents and reporting to the legislator. Ask to speak to the legislative assistant (L.A.) who handles education issues.

- State your interest clearly and briefly to the receptionist and you will be put through to the appropriate staff person.

- At the outset, restate your name, town, and the agency or organization that you represent (e.g., CEC, division, federation, chapter, etc.).

- Outline your concerns in a brief, yet orderly manner.

- State your reasons for support or opposition to the issue.

- Ask clear and precise questions.

- Do not keep the person on the phone for more than 5 or 10 minutes. If you have additional material to send, tell the staff when it will be sent.

- Always try to follow up your phone call with a letter.

- Request a follow-up from the office with the legislator's position on the bill.

- In addition to his or her office on Capitol Hill, every legislator has a district office located in your state. If you're concerned about making a lot of long-distance phone calls, it's just as effective to contact your legislator's district office.

 Source: *CEC Special Education Advocacy Handbook*, 1995, The Council for Exceptional Children.

Communicating By Telegram

There are times when speed of response, by those in the states, to legislators in Washington, DC is important. When this situation occurs, the telegram may be the best device to use to get the message to the Congress as quickly as possible.

Contact Western Union and inquire about their special rates for public reaction to legislative activities.

In addition to the telegram, other options at reduced rates include:

- Personal Opinion Message: Consists of up to 15 words, can be sent to any public official (you are not charged for names or addresses) and delivery occurs the same day the message is sent.

- Mailgram: Contains up to 100 words, can be sent to anyone. Delivery is by the U.S. Postal Service and arrives the day after the message is sent.

- Night Letter: Night letters of up to 100 words are sent at night and arrive the next day at a reduced rate.

- Most legislators have public FAX numbers. Send your message via FAX in either a letter or telegram format.

- Electronic mail: Most legislators have access to such technology as the Internet or Prodigy. Send them a message over the electronic highway!

Continuing Communications

Strive to develop a continuing communicative relationship with your legislator and his/her staff. This will counteract the legislator's possible impression that he or she hears from you only when you want something. Consider supplying information about disability issues throughout the year. If your information is consistently useful and dependable, the legislator will be encouraged to rely on it.

Other Methods of Getting to Know Your Legislators

The people who serve in our legislatures are usually reasonable people who will respond favorably to a logical and reasonable approach. Legislators are influenced not only by rational argument, but also by pragmatic concerns of politics (e.g., votes, party loyalties, etc.).

In addition to the methods described in the earlier sections of this handbook such as letters, telegrams, and phone calls, the following methods should also help in influencing legislation favorable to children and youth with exceptionalities and special education, in general.

1. **Attendance at hearings**

   Even if you are not testifying, attendance at relevant hearings will have an effective influence on legislative votes. The mere physical presence of impressive members of CEC could have critical impact on the outcome of getting important legislation passed.

2. **Political receptions and dinners**

   Meetings of the type at all levels of government are invaluable in getting to know legislators as well as their staff aides. When appropriate you may want to give an award (usually a plaque) to a legislator or a staff member for his or her efforts on behalf of special education and the disability community. Be sure to take pictures of the legislators and publish these in newsletters, journals, etc. A copy of these should be sent to the individual. In addition, a good turnout of CEC members for a dinner or reception demonstrates a show of strength and a high level of interest in special education matters.

Source: *CEC Special Education Advocacy Handbook*, 1995, The Council for Exceptional Children.

Dinners may be handled in a variety of ways: you might have one legislator as the main speaker or you may have several officials where a particular bill or special education issue can be discussed. You might also consider general special education issues at such a meeting. In any event, a banquet, dinner, and so forth, is an excellent opportunity to interact on a one-to-one basis with legislators in a pleasant environment, removed from the formal atmosphere of the U.S. Capitol or State Capitals.

3. **Speaking engagements by legislators**

Invitations to speak to groups of constituents are usually welcomed by legislators, since such visits provide high visibility necessary in political life. Both the legislator and the constituents get a chance to exchange views. This type of event allows CEC members to express needs and their positions on specific legislation. It also gives visibility to the CEC unit. Once again, good preparation for any meeting with an elected official or officials is essential. CEC members should clearly know their agenda. If a legislator should ask for information that is not available at the dinner, be sure to follow-up within a few days with the requested materials. The response should reference the event (e.g., banquet, dinner, etc.).

4. **Setting up site visits**

Nothing can provide a positive message to legislators better than children themselves! Set up a time for your legislator to visit your school or program, and allow him or her to see how effective special education can really be for students with exceptionalities.

Finally, have patience! Advocacy is usually a deliberate, painstaking process.

UNDERSTANDING THE REGULATORY PROCESS

Once your persistence and knowledge has paid off, and the law you've fought so hard for is enacted, your vigilance should not end there. Often, a law is intentionally vague, leaving it up to the overseeing regulatory agency to issue a rule that specifies the law's intent. For example, since the U.S. Department of Education's Office of Special Education and Rehabilitative Services (OSERS) is the agency in charge of implementing the Individuals with Disabilities Education Act (IDEA), that is the agency responsible for the development and monitoring of the law's regulations. Other federal regulatory agencies include the U.S. Department of Health and Human Services (HHS), the U.S. Department of Justice (DOJ), and the Equal Employment Opportunity Commission (EEOC).

There are many definitions of what a regulation is; however, most political scientists and economists generally agree on the following: first, regulation transfers some amount of private discretion to the public sector; and second, it entails sanctions to discourage undesired conduct.

Federal regulatory agencies use two procedures for writing and enforcing their regulations: adjudication and rule making. Adjudication is a process through which the agency deals with the activities of a specific company or companies. Rule making is a process used to write standards and regulations for products and services. When an agency wants to propose a rule, it must give general notice in the *Federal Register.*

The *Federal Register*

The *Federal Register* is the basic tool for finding out about agency rulings, proposed rules, meetings, and adjudicatory proceedings. The rules and regulations that appear daily in the *Register* are codified by subject title in the *Code of Federal Regulations* (CFR), which is updated annually. Documents contained in the *Register* are arranged under one of five headings: "Presidential Documents," "Proposed Rules," "Rules and Regulations," "Notices," and "Sunshine Meetings."

Source: *CEC Special Education Advocacy Handbook,* 1995, The Council for Exceptional Children.

Proposed Rules

The format for publishing a proposed rule is as follows: The entry contains a brief description of the action; the nature of the action (proposed rule making, extension of public comment period, etc.); a summary of the proposed rule; the deadlines for receiving public comments and/or dates of public hearings; and a detailed supplementary section. An "advance notice of proposed rule making" is published in cases where a rule is being considered but the agency had not developed a concrete proposal.

Rules and Regulations

With a few exceptions, federal agencies are required to publish final rules and regulations in the *Federal Register* 30 days before they are to take effect. Each entry in this section usually contains a descriptive heading of the change, the type of action involved (e.g., a final rule, a termination of rule making or proceeding, a request for further public comment); a brief summary of the nature of the action; and the effective date. This is followed by supplementary information, including the text of the change in the regulation. The supplementary information on final rules must summarize comments received about the rule, what action was taken on them, and why.

Notices

This section contains documents other than rules or proposed rules that are applicable to the public. Notices of hearings and investigations, committee meetings, and agency decisions and rulings are examples.

Sunshine Meetings

Notice of open agency meetings are printed in the *Federal Register*. Each entry contains the agency's name; time, date, and place of the meeting; a brief description of the subject; and supplementary information.

Getting Involved

Once a law has been passed, you should offer your assistance and guidance to the agency that will promulgate the regulations for the Act, to help make sure that the regulations appropriately reflect the law's intent. Respond to the call for public comment during the proposed rule stage, whether it be orally or in written comment form. You might also want to attend the open agency meetings that are announced in the *Register*. That way, you can stay abreast of the issues that the agency is and will be focusing on.

Understanding the structure of the Offices and Divisions in the Department of Education, both at federal and state levels, will help you advocate on behalf of the profession and of children with exceptionalities. Knowing who oversees what areas will allow you to make quick contacts with persons who are skilled in your particular area of concern. Often, agency personnel have a good feel for the special education climate and may be able to provide insight as to which groups or individuals may support or oppose your goals.

For an organization chart highlighting the offices within the U.S. Department of Education, or a detailed breakdown of the Office of Special Education Programs (OSEP), which is within OSERS, please contact the Department of Public Policy.

Source: *CEC Special Education Advocacy Handbook*, 1995, The Council for Exceptional Children.

HOW TO ACCESS THE MEDIA

Media advocacy is the strategic use of mass media as a resource for advancing social or public policy change. Like advocacy in general, media advocacy is an art. Most of what the great masters of media advocacy have learned, they discovered through experience.

The limitations of this handbook apply to media as they apply to advocacy in general. That is, this is not a cookbook; it cannot offer specific formulas for solving the problems you will encounter. But it can suggest approaches, ways of using the media as a resource, and an important element of your advocacy campaign.

Media gatekeepers are much like policymakers. Both have limited time and attention, so both must be lobbied effectively to get what you want from them. Don't ever wait to be contacted by members of the media. When you want them to cover a story, take an activist approach. As with politicians, the easier you can make a reporter's job (e.g., the more work you can do for him/her), the better. This is especially true when it comes to framing your issues. Work hard to put the bare facts of your story into the framework or perspective in which you want them viewed.

Always remember that media is a means to an end, never an end in itself. The media can sometimes function like a mind-altering drug; the quest for coverage can overpower the well-meaning advocate and cause him/her to lose sight of his/her immediate and long-term goals. Remember that bad coverage can do more harm than no coverage at all. Do not get caught up in the power of the media. It is only one of the many weapons you will use in the battle for reform. The emphasis is on using it, not letting it use you.

Source: *CEC Special Education Advocacy Handbook,* 1995, The Council for Exceptional Children.

What's CEC Newsworthy?

This *Handbook* provides general tips on how to access and use the media to your best advantage. But how do you know what issues the press will really respond to and want to give coverage to? And what should your main goals be in your interactions with the media? Here are some guidelines:

Your Four CEC PR Goals

- To serve the goal of improving educational outcomes for students with exceptionalities.

- To heighten the visibility, understanding, and appreciation of special educators.

- To increase CEC membership.

- To increase the recruitment of persons into the special education profession.

Is It News?

One of these three elements can be found in stories that get press coverage:

- Increasing public awareness—By increasing public awareness of the truth, you provide a balanced view of the issues at stake. Stories can expose the peril of the alternatives or provide solutions.

- Solutions to a problem—When your product or service (e.g., membership/conference) provides a solution to a problem or meets the needs of an audience, publicity can be generated.

- Responding as an expert—Press will seek you out when you are perceived as being a credible expert in a field.

Your story ideas can relate to the following as well: current events, recognized achievement, area of influence, large interest base, human interest, milestones, controversy, personal significance, or neighborhood factors.

Media Strategies

A media strategy is a plan for using the media to accomplish a specific goal. To be successful, a media strategy must be carefully thought out and tailored to accomplish its goal. In particular, the strategist must know:

- **What the goal is, in precise and realistic terms.**

- **What the message is, in clear, simple terms.**

- **Who the target audience is.**

- **What outlets are best to disseminate the message and reach the target audience.**

- **What the audience should do after they have heard the message.**

- **What assistance will be needed to accomplish the goal.**

As in all successful advocacy interventions, a good media strategy requires you to stick to a single central theme. Make your total message revolve around it. Keep the theme simple and appealing.

It's important that you involve CEC leadership in determining your media strategy, making sure to include your federation/division (or chapter) president, your membership/program chair, and your PAN Coordinator or government relations liaison. Together, you should decide what issues your unit will focus on, and what your message(s) will be.

Media Relations/Public Relations

You should form personal relationships with state/local reporters that will be mutually beneficial. You need them, but they also need you.

Become as familiar with the many different media outlets in your area as you can. Learn their format, style, and the demographics of their audience.

Compared to electronic reporters, print reporters:

- **have more time;**

- **are able to get more deeply into their stories;**

- **are more anonymous;**

- **make much less money.**

It is best to contact members of the media when you do not want something specific from them. (For example, you could arrange a meeting with the editorial board of your local newspaper before your issue gets hot.) Take the time to introduce yourself, your organization, and your cause. Let them know that you are an expert on your issues, and become a continuing resource for them. Build the mutual trust and respect that are essential to all successful relationships.

But always remember that reporters' interests will not always converge with yours. They are after stories, not social goals. Therefore, if the goal can be related to a specific local program or issue, the "story" line can evolve while still delivering the message about the issue. It is your responsibility to package the information that you give them in a way that serves both your and their needs. Don't count on anything you say being truly "off the record." If you never want to see it in print, don't say it.

As in political advocacy, a good rule of thumb in media advocacy is that there are no permanent friends and no permanent enemies.

Keep track of the reporters on your "beat." Learn all you can about who makes the decisions in each media outlet and how. Newspapers have reporters, but they also have section editors, city editors, national editors, feature editors, managing editors, and publishers. Broadcast

Source: *CEC Special Education Advocacy Handbook*, 1995, The Council for Exceptional Children.

personnel include assignment managers, planning editors, and executive producers. The key people in each outlet are worth meeting in person.

Never, never lie or mislead a reporter. Information is the commodity you are marketing, but credibility is what you must use to sell it. Exaggeration is not necessary when it comes to issues regarding children and youth with exceptionalities.

As mentioned before, focus your attentions on local media, whether it be print or electronic. CEC Headquarters' staff is typically the contact for national press. If you have an issue or event in your area that warrants national attention, contact CEC's Department of Public Policy or the Department of Marketing and Public Relations.

Develop a local targeted media network—start with a goal of a dozen names, targeting your main audiences. In addition, coordinate your efforts with your president and PAN Coordinator if possible. Build your media network so that it includes the following:

* The Council for Exceptional Children (for *TEACHING Exceptional Children, CEC Today*, and so that Headquarters can disseminate it nationally to CEC units, and national press/stakeholders).

* Local news media.

* Local education/disability associations.

* Local and state education agency vehicles, both special and general education publications.

Accessing the Media

Media is a limited resource. Access is reserved for those stories which media managers deem to be newsworthy—for example, significant, interesting, and new. Therefore, advocates must look constantly for new ways to push their issue. These opportunities for access are called news "pegs," "angles," or "hooks."

Factors that get people to pay attention to a news story are the traditional criteria for news:

- **Timeliness. News, by definition, is new.**

- **Proximity. The event is within the audience's perception of their community.**

- **Consequence. The news will affect the viewer/reader.**

- **Human interest. An appeal to emotion or an illustration of a universal truth.**

- **Conflict. A clash of opposing interests.**

- **Prominence. Such as associations with a celebrity or renowned figure.**

- **Unusualness. Something that has not happened before.**

Some other, nontraditional definitions of news are:

- **Inoffensiveness. The media not only does not want to offend anyone, they want to avoid public complaint. This gives vocal, mobilized segments of the public a disproportional amount of influence with the media.**

- **Congruence. If the information is too unusual, if it does not fit society's existing theoretical constructs, it will not sell.**

- **Brevity. Whether broadcast or printed, information has to be packaged into short bites and compete with the clutter of other bits of information.**

Source: *CEC Special Education Advocacy Handbook*, 1995, The Council for Exceptional Children.

To be successful at media advocacy, you must remain flexible and responsive. Seize whatever opportunities present themselves to push your issues. In this sense, a media advocacy campaign is like a political campaign in which candidates react constantly to unexpected events and late-breaking news.

You can piggyback local coverage on national events, such as National Disability Week, CEC's Exceptional Children's Week, CEC's national convention held every year in April, or your federation/division/local conference. Always try to give your story a local spin.

You will find more avenues to access the media by thinking of different ways to package your information. Hard news is what is reported on the front page of the newspaper and on the 6 p.m. news. Coverage of hard news is very limited, because hard news stories are tersely written. However, alternatives to hard news coverage are called soft news. They include feature stories, human interest stories, individual profiles, and what is in the lifestyle section of the newspaper.

Do not hesitate to call a reporter if you think you have a good story. Remember that they are paid to gather news from informants like yourself.

Following are some ways of accessing the media on paper:

- Issue a written **calendar or event advisory** far in advance of the event. This can be faxed or even hand-delivered.

- Issue a **press release.** This is best for print media, with lots of lead time and limited in-house reporting resources. Should be written so it could be reprinted directly or with few changes.

- Mail or fax a **"tickler,"** which is a one-page, informal presentation of ideas or angles on stories that do not have particular deadlines. The tickler should be accompanied by substantial background information.

- A **pitch letter** is sent to a specific journalist who will be interested in the story. This letter, which often sells the story, should be personalized; this is a great way to build a relationship with a reporter. When you make initial contact by mail, follow up with phone calls.

Ask the reporter if he or she is on a deadline (they almost always are!). If so, ask when it would be convenient for you to call back. If they're not on deadline, ask if you can have 30 seconds of their time.

Keep good records of your contacts with the press and their responses. You may want to contact them again.

Remember local radio talk show hosts and local cable stations. They have commitments to their own communities and a lot of time to fill each day.

Be proactive and assertive in accessing the media. Other ways to do so include:

- **News Briefings:** Use an informal news briefing when you have sufficient lead time (e.g., 30 days) before a news event, when the issue is complex, and when reporters would benefit from advance notice and good background information. Briefings can be held with individual reporters or small groups.

- **News Conference:** Hold a news conference only if you have hard news and cannot handle the story in any other way (e.g., through a simple press release). The fanciest trappings of a news conference cannot create or add to the substance of any story. The worst result is an event that no one attends, or one from which no one takes a story. Make sure you had a valid reason to hold a news conference; for example, hold one in conjunction with your local or state CEC conference, your overall advocacy efforts, or your celebration in honor of CEC's Exceptional Children's Week.

- **Feature a Good Speaker:** The spokesperson should deliver a statement, but must also be prepared to engage in open dialogue with the press.

- **Use good audio/visual materials.**

- **Distribute press kits at the event** that include background information, biographies, and other useful materials. Press kits may also include general CEC information/overview; leadership informa-

Source: *CEC Special Education Advocacy Handbook, 1995*, The Council for Exceptional Children.

tion; division/state/provincial/federation/chapter information; press clips; calendar of events; current and future programs; newsletters/ journals; and information about unmet needs (e.g., importance of resources to the education of our students, special education fact sheets).

For more information and guidance about accessing the media, get a copy of CEC's *Public Relations Survival Guide.* To order your copy, call the Department of Marketing and Public Relations at CEC Headquarters, 703/264-9462.

Media Presentations/Interviews

Whether you're being interviewed by a reporter over the phone, or you get scheduled to appear on a local radio or television show, follow the same approach as in giving testimony in a hearing.

Before each show and each interview (live or recorded), find out as much about the format as you can, especially how much time you will have. Learn as much as you can about the audience, too. If you have the opportunity, assist the reporter in developing the questions you will be asked. Provide background information, including facts and figures that might be useful to the reporter (and to your own cause).

Keep language simple and direct. Don't use jargon. Jargon puts people off. Speak in short, clear, punchy (e.g., quotable) sentences. Pretaped interviews will be edited, so points that are made in long, rambling paragraphs will be lost. Remember that much of what you say will be reduced to 15-second sound bites.

Make your most important point first. If you try leading up to it with background information, you may not get it in at all, or you may lose your audience in the meantime.

Be prepared with short, well-phrased explanations of your main points, but be attentive throughout the interview so you can respond to what is being said.

Emphasize your major points by "flagging" or listing them. (Example: "The most important thing to remember is …" "The three crucial conclusions are …")

Maintain control throughout the interview. Do not feel compelled to answer a question if you don't like it. Rather, use it as an opportunity to get your point across. Be ready to "reframe" questions that are off the mark.

Prepare three memorized objectives, or sound bites, that you can always refer to if the interview strays a bit. You can "bridge back" to these points if a reporter tries to get you to say something that is contrary to CEC's objectives. For example, if the reporter says that another special education agency offered a different perspective on an issue, and

Source: *CEC Special Education Advocacy Handbook*, 1995, The Council for Exceptional Children.

asks you to comment, instead of out-and-out refuting that organization's opinion, say "Well, that may be their point of view. But CEC feels that ..."

Don't try to be a know-it-all. If you don't have the answer to a particular question, don't fake it. Instead, use the opportunity to make one of your main points, or, if time allows, offer to find the information the reporter wants.

Be patient, not belligerent; kind, not nasty; helpful, not argumentative. Let your expertise come across, but do not be haughty. Calmly "bridge" to your three sound bites. The audience will not retain the facts and figures you present, but they will remember how they feel about you.

THE LEGISLATIVE WORKSHOP

The best method for preparing people to advocate for special education policy interests is to hold a legislative workshop or a series of workshops tailored to meet specific national- or state-oriented activities. Following are four types of workshops:

1. **The Basic Legislative Workshop**

    As the title implies, this is the type of program that reviews the basic information needed to prepare a CEC member to become a grass-roots advocate. In addition, this basic session should help motivate and stimulate the person's interest about the importance of the legislative process in serving the needs of children and youth with exceptionalities. This latter fact cannot be given enough emphasis.

The Format of a Basic Legislative Workshop

This *Handbook* can easily serve as the basis for this type of legislative workshop. Each section has useful guidelines and tips for use by CEC members at all levels of government, whether it be federal, state, or local. It is suggested that the workshop leader have some real experiences in grass-roots advocacy. In addition, the program should feature a legislator or legislative staff person as a speaker or participant. This approach will sustain interest as well as add credibility to the workshop. At the basic workshop (and all other types of workshops to be described in this *Handbook*), the following form should be used to ascertain the CEC member's potential for involvement in legislative matters. This form should be sent to workshop participants in advance of the program and returned to the workshop leader prior to the meeting. The information will help the leader ascertain the level of involvement with legislators, aid him or her in developing strategies, and determine how to best utilize these individuals in establishing or maintaining a legislative action committee.

Source: *CEC Special Education Advocacy Handbook,* 1995, The Council for Exceptional Children.

Legislative Information Form

1. Indicate the names and telephone numbers of the following elected officials:
    National level: Your two U.S. Senators

    _____

    _____

    U.S. House of Representatives (from your congressional district)

    _____

    Be sure to list the Washington, DC telephone number and the home office number.

    _____

2. Indicate the names of the State Senators and Representatives from your home state and districts.

3. Check to see which committees/subcommittees your elected officials (both federal and state) serve on. It is especially important to know which legislators are on the committees associated with appropriations, education, health, and child welfare.

4. Note the names of any legislators with whom you are close personal friends, business friends, or have ties to through another friend or relative.

5. Develop a list of CEC members that you could call upon to assist with telephone calls or letters to legislators.

6. List any coalitions that you are currently associated with concerning special education or other issues.

7. Have you ever held political office? (If yes, describe.)

    _____

This **Legislative Information Form** can be expanded to meet individual state needs by simply substituting your state senators and representatives in place of your federal Congressmen. The information can also be useful in a brief discussion on developing key contacts in government.

Source: *CEC Special Education Advocacy Handbook*, 1995, The Council for Exceptional Children.

65

2. **Special Orientation Workshop**

In this type of workshop, the focus might be on any issue or set of legislative initiatives that are current or pending at a level of government. In this instance, a speaker or panel could be used to inform and discuss the pros and cons of the issue. The workshop agenda could also include the development of new or different language for the bills under scrutiny.

The conclusion of this workshop could include several resolutions about the bill that should be delivered to the appropriate members of the House and Senate.

Such a workshop might also focus on action steps or strategies to be taken on behalf of a specific bill.

3. **A Workshop Combining Basic Information As Well As a Special Orientation to Some Current Issue**

This type of workshop combines the elements of both Workshops 1 and 2 just described. For this workshop, extremely careful planning is necessary for obvious reasons. It is assumed that if giving basic information, you are dealing with newcomers to advocacy. At the same time, you may also be discussing plans and strategies for developing a response to a new Senate bill.

In this case, it is important to move slowly with the information to avoid fear and confusion about the roles to be played by the workshop attendees. Be sure at least a third of the audience has some hands-on experience with some aspect of grass-roots advocacy. This combination will provide for more meaningful discussion and help build needed confidence in the less informed members. Role models are important in learning the legislative/advocacy procedures.

4. **A Workshop on How to Access the Media**

This type of workshop could be presented either separately or in addition to any of the workshops just listed. While it is important to have an understanding of the basic legislative issues involved in

Source: *CEC Special Education Advocacy Handbook*, 1995, The Council for Exceptional Children.

grass-roots advocacy, it is equally important to have a working knowledge of how and when to use the media to your best advantage.

For this workshop, the agenda could include an overview of media strategies, as presented in this *Handbook,* followed by practical input and advice from advocates who have real-life experience in dealing with the media. In addition, representatives from a variety of media sources could serve on a panel to discuss the kinds of issues they're interested in covering.

Bibliography

Advocacy Institute. (1990). *The elements of a successful public interest advocacy campaign.* Washington, DC: Author.

Andreasen, N. C. (1984). *The broken brain: The biological revolution in psychiatry.* New York: Harper and Row.

Congressional Quarterly. (1988). *How a bill becomes a law.* Washington, DC: Author.

Congressional Quarterly. *Regulation process and politics.* Washington, DC: Author.

The Council for Exceptional Children. (1994). *Public relations survival guide.* Reston, VA: Author.

Hamilton, J. L., & Safer, N. D. (1992). Single subject research and the policy process. *Advances in learning and behavioral disabilities* (Vol. 7) (pp. 291-309). Greenwich, CT: JAI Press, Inc.

Klein, T., & Danzig, F. (1974, 1985). *Publicity: How to make the media work for you.* New York: Charles Scribner's.

Langkau, T. J. (1988). *Promoting voting: A citizen's guide to media.* Washington, DC: American Citizenship Education Project.

Meredith, J. C., & Myer, L. (1982). *Lobbying on a shoestring: How to win in Massachusetts ... and other places, too.* Boston: Massachusetts Poverty Law Center.

Meyer P. *Factors that affect media responsiveness to public health.*

National Rehabilitation Association. (1993). *Handbook for Rehabilitation Advocacy.* Alexandria: Author.

Wittenberg, E., & Wittenberg, E. (1989). *How to win in Washington: Very practical advice about lobbying, the grassroots, and the media.* Cambridge, MA: Basil Blackwell, Inc.

Wolpe, B. C. (1990). *Lobbying Congress: How the system works.* Washington, DC: The Congressional Quarterly.

The Council for Exceptional Children wishes to acknowledge and thank the National Rehabilitation Association, from which portions of the information in this *Handbook* were adapted.

GLOSSARY OF LEGISLATIVE TERMS

Act—technically, the designation of a bill after it has passed one house of Congress. Also used as a synonym for law. The term for legislation that has passed both houses of Congress and has been signed by the President or passed over his veto.

Amendment—proposal of a member of Congress to alter the language or stipulations in a bill or act. It is usually printed, debated, and voted upon in the same manner as a bill.

Appropriation Bill—permits the expenditure of the monies approved by an authorization bill, but usually not to the total permissible under the authorizing legislation. An appropriation bill originates in the House and normally is not acted on until its authorization measure is enacted.

Authorization Bill—legislation setting up or continuing programs; sets general aims and purposes and may set a ceiling for funding. Usually enacted before appropriation bill is passed.

Bill—legislative proposal introduced in either house (until it has been passed by that House). Designated HR (House of Representatives) or S (Senate) according to the house in which it originates and by a number assigned in the order which it is introduced.

Budget—document sent to Congress by the President in January of each year estimating revenues and expenditures for the ensuing fiscal year.

Calendars—arrangements for scheduling legislative business.

House:	Union	— bills for revenue and appropriations
	House	— other public bills
	Private	— bills pertaining to individual or private interests
	Consent	— controversial bills
	Discharge	— motions to discharge from committee

Senate: Legislative — all bills

Executive — items under advise and consent power

Clean Bill—after a committee has considered and revised a bill, it may rewrite it incorporating its amendments into a new or "clean bill." This bill is given a new number and is the committee's best judgment of superior sections in all versions.

Closed Rule—(House) prohibits the offering of amendments, thus requiring that the bill be accepted or rejected as reported by committee.

Cloture—a process by which debate can be ended in the Senate. A motion for cloture requires 16 senators' signatures for introduction and support of two-thirds of those present and voting.

Committee—a subdivision of the House or Senate which prepares legislation for action by the parent chamber or makes investigations as directed by the parent chamber. There are several types of committees. Most standing committees are divided into subcommittees, which study legislation, hold hearings, and report their recommendations to the full committee. Only the full committee can report legislation for action by the House or Senate.

Committee of the Whole—when the House sits as one committee to consider legislation reported by a standing committee before it goes to the floor; the committee debates and amends legislation. Requires only 100 members for a quorum.

Committee Report—written explanation and justification for recommendations submitted by committee to full chamber after the committee has scrutinized and decided to favorably report a bill. Used by courts, executive departments, and the public as a source of information on the purpose and meaning of a law.

Conference Committee—a committee made up of members from both houses; purpose is to iron out differences between House and Senate versions of a bill.

Source: *CEC Special Education Advocacy Handbook,* 1995, The Council for Exceptional Children.

Congressional Record—daily record of the proceedings and debates of Senate and House versions of a bill.

Continuing Appropriation—when a fiscal year begins and Congress has not yet enacted all the regular appropriation bills for that year, it passes a joint resolution "continuing appropriations" for government agencies at rates generally based on its previous year's appropriations.

Expenditures—the actual spending of money as distinguished from the appropriation of it. Expenditures are made by the disbursing officers of the administration; appropriations are made only by Congress. The two are rarely identical in any fiscal year; expenditures may represent money appropriated 1, 2, or more years previously.

Hearings—committee session for hearing witnesses. At hearings on legislation, witnesses usually include floor spokesman for their party. This person is elected by party caucus.

Pigeonhole—shelving a bill without a final vote; usually refers to blockage by a committee; allows a bill to die by failure of a committee to act.

Privileged Bills—(House) bills that have precedence over normal order of business and do not require Rules Committee action; reports from Committee on Appropriations on general appropriation bills and reports from Committee on Ways and Means on bills raising revenue are privileged bills.

Quorum—number of members who must be present to conduct business; in the House it is 218 and in the Senate it is 51.

Ranking Member—member of a committee who has more seniority on the committee than any other member of his party. Usually used in reference to the most senior minority party member.

Recession—an item in an appropriation bill rescinding, or canceling, funds previously appropriated but not spent. Also, the repeal of a previous appropriation by the President to cut spending, if approved by Congress under procedures in the Budget and Impoundment Control Act of 1974.

Report—both a verb and a noun, as a congressional **term. A committee that has been** examining a bill referred to it by **the parent chamber "reports"** its findings and recommendations **to the chamber when the committee returns the measure. The process is called "reporting" a bill.**

A "report" is the document setting forth the committee's explanation of its action. House and Senate reports are numbered separately and are designated S. Rept. or H. Rept. Conference reports are numbered and designated in the same way as regular committee reports.

Most reports favor a bill's passage. Adverse reports are occasionally submitted, but more often, when a committee disapproves a bill, it simply fails to report it at all. When a committee report is not unanimous, the dissenting committee members may file a statement of their views, called minority views and referred to as a minority report. Sometimes a bill is reported without recommendation.

Rider—an amendment proposing substantive legislation attached to another bill.

Seniority—refers to length of uninterrupted service in Congress and specifically on a committee; criterion usually used for determining committee chairmanships.

Session—normally, each Congress consists of two sessions, usually beginning in January and ending when Congress adjourns for the year.

Standing Committee—committee whose existence is permanent and continuing from one Congress to the next; there are 21 in the House and 17 in the Senate.

Subcommittee—smaller subject-matter divisions of a committee; facilitates specialization and division of labor.

Supplemental Appropriations—normally are passed after the regular (annual) appropriations bills, but before the end of fiscal year to which they apply. Also referred to as "deficiencies."

Source: *CEC Special Education Advocacy Handbook*, 1995, The Council for Exceptional Children.

Suspension of the Rules—in the House a two-thirds majority may suspend the rules and bring a bill directly to the floor; in the Senate, **only a majority vote is needed.**

Teller Votes—(House) taken in Committee by the Whole by counting congressmen for or against a measure as they walk down the aisle; (until the Legislative Reorganization Act of 1970, there was not a provision for recording teller votes).

Unanimous Consent—usual way of conducting business in the Senate; after morning hour, majority leader asks unanimous consent to consider pending legislation; such requests are rarely objected to; also used in both houses in lieu of a vote on noncontroversial measures.

Veto—action by the President if he doesn't approve of a bill or joint resolution; he returns it with his objections to the house of origin and the bill may be reconsidered; must receive approval of two-thirds of both chambers to become law. When Congress has adjourned, the President may pocket veto a bill by refusing to sign it.

Whip—chosen by party caucus as an assistant to the floor leader; job is to keep in touch with all members of his party, discover their voting intentions, and get them to the floor for a vote.

Source: *CEC Special Education Advocacy Handbook*, 1995, The Council for Exceptional Children.

You are already an accomplished advocate!

Source: *CEC Special Education Advocacy Handbook,* 1995, The Council for Exceptional Children.

75

(Overhead for pg. 6)

Stages in Influencing the Policy Process

1) **Involve the policymaker when trying to effect change.**

2) **Make sure your reasons for change are sound.**

3) **Your information MUST be timely and appropriate.**

4) **Present your information in the most effective way possible.**

What Makes Politicians Tick

- **Politicians hold public office to help others.**

- **Politicians like to be asked for help.**

- **Politicians are good learners.**

- **Politicians do not know everything!**

- **Politicians have many demands on their time.**

- **Politicians do not have sufficient resources to meet demands made on them.**

- **Politicians are always running for office.**

Source: *CEC Special Education Advocacy Handbook*, 1995, The Council for Exceptional Children.

79

What Makes Politicians Tick (pg. 2)

- Politicians respond to crises.

- Politicians behave differently when they know they're being watched.

- Politicians like to be thanked.

- Politicians love good press!

Source: *CEC Special Education Advocacy Handbook*, 1995, The Council for Exceptional Children.

81

"The Cardinal Rule for Every Encounter with Every Community Leader, Politician, and Media Gatekeeper is to BE PLEASANT!"

Source: *CEC Special Education Advocacy Handbook,* 1995, The Council for Exceptional Children.

83

Rules for Effective Advocacy

1) Ask for what you want.

2) Be specific in your request.

3) Be ready to work hard.

4) Find a legislative champion.

5) Organize, coordinate, orchestrate.

6) Touch all the bases.

7) Stay flexible, be opportunistic.

8) Keep it simple.

Source: *CEC Special Education Advocacy Handbook*, 1995, The Council for Exceptional Children.

Rules for Effective Advocacy (pg. 2)

9) Assume the perspective of others.

10) Build and preserve your credibility.

11) Anticipate and deal with your opposition.

12) Be prepared to compromise.

13) Never burn your bridges.

14) Target your efforts.

15) Honor the staff.

16) Track your progress.

17) Be persistent.

18) Follow up.

Source: *CEC Special Education Advocacy Handbook*, 1995, The Council for Exceptional Children.

A coalition is a union of people or organizations seeking similar ends.

Coalitions are centralized and hierarchical.

Source: *CEC Special Education Advocacy Handbook*, 1995, The Council for Exceptional Children.

89

(Overhead for pg. 23)

Networks have NO formal leadership structure.

Source: *CEC Special Education Advocacy Handbook*, 1995, The Council for Exceptional Children.

(Overhead for pg. 27)

Information is never received in a vacuum.

Source: *CEC Special Education Advocacy Handbook,* 1995, The Council for Exceptional Children.

93

(Overhead for pg. 34)

Hearings function to create a public record.

They present a great opportunity to advocate your position.

Source: *CEC Special Education Advocacy Handbook,* 1995, The Council for Exceptional Children.

Tips To Be Used For Testimony

1) Identify yourself and your organization.

2) State your position.

3) Summarize your recommendations first, then explain them.

4) Sum up your position.

5) Prepare enough copies of your testimony.

6) Avoid cliches, wordiness, generalities, and flattery.

7) Be clear, concise, and brief.

8) Use plain English and avoid jargon.

Source: *CEC Special Education Advocacy Handbook*, 1995, The Council for Exceptional Children.

(Overhead for pg. 48)

Other Ways to Get to Know Your Legislator

- **Attendance at a hearing**

- **Political receptions and dinners**

- **Speaking engagements by legislators**

- **Setting up site visits**

Source: *CEC Special Education Advocacy Handbook,* 1995, The Council for Exceptional Children.

Media advocacy is the strategic use of mass media as a resource for advancing social or public policy change.

Source: *CEC Special Education Advocacy Handbook*, 1995, The Council for Exceptional Children.

(Overhead for pg. 54)

Your Four CEC PR Goals

- To serve the goal of improving educational outcomes for students with exceptionalities

- To heighten the visibility, understanding, and appreciation of special educators

- To increase CEC membership

- To increase the recruitment of persons into the special education profession

Source: *CEC Special Education Advocacy Handbook,* 1995, The Council for Exceptional Children.

(Overhead for pg. 56)

Don't count on anything you say being truly "off the record."

If you never want to see it in print, don't say it!

Source: *CEC Special Education Advocacy Handbook*, 1995, The Council for Exceptional Children.